OUTSWIMMING THE ERUPTION

ALLAN CROSBIE

OUTSWIMMING THE ERUPTION

A *The Rialto*
First Edition

ACKNOWLEDGEMENTS

Poems from this collection, or early versions of them, have appeared in the following publications: *BBC Wildlife Magazine; Cencrastus; Chapman; The Daily Telegraph; Edinburgh: An Intimate City; Fife Lines; Groundswell (Edinburgh University); The Interpreter's House; Magistri Pro Pace; The Mallard Poetry Competition Anthology 1998; New Welsh Review; New Writing Scotland; Northwords; Orbis; Poetry Life; Poetry Scotland; The Rialto; Southfields; Stand.*

'América' was a runner-up in the 1998 Arvon/Daily Telegraph Poetry competition and published in *Ring of Words*, the competition anthology, along with 'Camping on the Fault'.

'The House Swap', first published in the *Interpreter's House*, was short-listed for the Forward Prize for Best Individual Poem in 2001 and later published in the *Forward Book of Poetry 2002*.

The author gratefully acknowledges the support of the Scottish Arts Council in the form of a Writer's Bursary in 1999.

The author wishes to thank Colin Finlayson, Jack Hamilton and Alex Wallace, and the community of James Gillespie's High School, for supporting his attendance at an Arvon course in 1998, and a three month leave of absence in 2000.

Thanks also to the following poets for advice and encouragement at different times in the past ten years: Ron Butlin, Stewart Conn, Robert Crawford, Douglas Dunn, Don Paterson, Alastair Reid, and all members of Edinburgh's Shore Poets.

First Published in 2006

The Rialto, PO Box 309, Aylsham, Norwich, England NR11 6LN

ISBN 09527444-9-X

The publisher acknowledges financial assistance from the Arts Council of England, East.

The Rialto is a Registered Charity No. 297553

Typeset in Berling Roman 10pt on 13pt leading

Design by Starfish, Norwich (www.starfishlimited.com)

Cover image courtesy of Oleg Pokrovsky (www.mountain.ru)

Printed by Printing Services (Norwich) Limited

For Ali

CONTENTS

THE VIEW FROM JENNERS

The dead umbrellas on the pavement bare
their broken ribs to the rain. Their flaps of skin
salute the wind that killed them, threw off their wings
and snapped their spines. They lie where they fell, abandoned,
cast behind backs, scattered black puddles
on Princes Street, tramped by the crowds battling
the storm or seeking refuge in M. and S. and Jenners.
Let's take that sanctuary and cast a quick glance
backwards through the door which swings
with a slowing flick and shush. The view is bleak
beyond the pavement's trashy casualties, the street
like hammered lead, the hissing traffic like shuttles
on a crazy loom. The rain obscures everything beyond,
so let's go in and shoulder through the crowds
and make-up counters (where over-glittered women
in heels and uniforms wrap gifts in tape that just
repeatsrepeatsrepeats the name they work for,
where perfume masks the pheromones it seeks
to emulate and proves while man-made scents
might seem like feminine allures their deepest nature's
sexless which men call sexy, being malapropellered
creatures) to The Proper Jenners, an Edinburgh
in miniature. The expanse of the hall is the hauteur
of the New Town, George Street parading itself,
the width of arrogance and leisure. But turn a corner,
climb a stair, and you're in a close, a nook,
where when you glance across or down or up
you see the place you left, and catch a glimpse
of you about to turn the corner you just turned.
And this is surely Old Town spookiness,
its secret cobbled byways, its canny short-cuts
to loss of self and sanity. This is the maze no string
can get you out of, this is the hall of mirrors
where inspiration comes but vanishes if you don't
grab a hold of yourself. (Take the poet
who composed his fable here of Scottish prophets
failing in their mission, and of their missing *faithers*,

The Temptation, which ends with a suicide's dying-moment
memory: as a child, lost in a department store
between two facing mirrors, cloned and trapped
in the endless corridor like a carriage in a train forever
rounding bends, dizzying and sick, he prays
his father will come, rising up from the pools
within pools behind him, to cup the back of his head
in his palm. And he does...) What is it about poets
and facing mirrors? And trains! Typical symbols,
hard and sleek and thrusting, of the need to penetrate
a surface and a tunnel, the need for the arrival's final
arrow-shower? We need other theories
for trains and stations. Waverley's a womb-Sargasso,
for example, and trains themselves give birth
to human litters into cities – their deepest
nature's feminine, as symbols tend to be
when you look beyond the obvious. The Scott Monument's
a good example – forget the sooty rocket
aimed at clouds, forget the needle stuck
through junked-up veins of Edinburgh's sick
and dying body: this is the tail-end of a Nessie
from Nor Loch's prehistoric past, petrified
Pompeii-style mid-dive, trying to outswim
the eruption, mid-birth of an egg whose shell's dissolved
and left this fossilised embryo, the statue, a Scottish
genius who's never quite delivered, caught
forever in that frozen monster's birth-canal,
the apex of the tail its mausoleum. There are more,
of course, but let's stay with children for the moment,
and swimming monsters, and recall that classic,
The Epic Adventures of the Fiji Mermaid
(a monkey/fish which swims from Tuvalu
to Struay and inspires a curriculum adviser
somewhere South to set a research project
on the creature's biochemistry and patterns of migration
and how it will adapt to Katie-Morag's
people and their culture). And let's see those diatribes
like **Progress of the Parliament**, or **Timeline** which begins –
– Sorry. You're right. Perhaps we'd better not.
You're getting bored? Tired of these displays?

Is it time to shut up shop and head for home?
What about that b.l.t. in Kennington's?
No? Lingerie? Or bridal wear? Just kidding.
Well, let's be going then, even though
we know this cannot be the end. For it always ends
at midnight when everything unlocks that shouldn't,
and the lioness comes padding from her cage and down
Corstorphine Road and past the dead umbrellas
like crumb-trails through the woods. With the slightest jump
she's rampant through the door which swings with a slowing
flick and shush. And shush! She's stalking through the counters –
with a pause to spray her scent at *Lancome, Calvin*
Klein, Chanel – then slinking step by step
to the toys downstairs, then further down, and down,
and further still to where there are no floors
or departments, just the constant hunt for a prey
that's so elusive its presence is known only
by the slightest flick of its tail around a corner,
or its spoor on the cooling magma that reveals it's female
and heavy with child, or a child too weak and new
in the world to keep up with the rest of the herd.

EDINBURGH
after Francis Thomson

It was one of those ice-blue days in January,
when the air's so pure you can read the lines
written for miles across the sky by jets,
when I saw the invisible and touched the intangible:

I caught an angel by the wing
as I lifted the post on my doormat.
It smacked the air like a startled pigeon
but I held fast – *Just tell me something before you go!*

So it told me of the fish that soars to find the ocean
and the eagle that dives to find the sky.
But I wanted something closer to home.
So it joked about the traffic on the ladder to heaven

that rises from Waverley station. *Come on*, I said,
something important. But it escaped then
by distracting me, showing me from my window
the beams of light that cut the sky and fell

on nothing but the waves that walked across the Forth.

CORN ISLAND BLUES

The bad omens in Bluefields should have warned me –
the red sky in the morning drawing its curtain
over the slow boat from Rama; the drizzle
sticking its warm wet fingers up my nostrils;
and the Scottish links that drew me there
to the Caribbean butt-end of Nicaragua failing
to show themselves (no Campbells or Fifes
marched across the street to embrace me and ask
about the latest cultural exchanges
after the twinning with Edinburgh; just a man
the locals knew as Elvis, an ex-Contra
who told me after small-talk he'd voted
for de ONE, man, the UNO, y'know?).

The trip itself's a nightmare-blur: the churning sky;
hitting the Atlantic storm head-on;
the engine going dead and wave after wave
biting into the hull until darkness wrapped us in its cloth;
the cramps in my gut when we got there, eating
papaya seeds for a cure, black pellets, like gunshot,
peppering my shit for days; the constant rain;
the nights alone clutching a machete
as the dog-sized rats went on their manoeuvres;
waiting a week for a boat going home. . .

The clearest thing in my memory? A joke. On me.
The captain of the boat, as the ropes were freed and we chugged
across the bay where the bluff hid the storm,
asked me, *Is it a sin to kiss de land
in you' country?* I was puzzled. Stupid. *No. . .*
Tha's good! he cried. And the whole boat laughed.

PADRE ANGEL

Like a scrawny hen this old Spanish priest
pouts and worries at his stubble, fidgets
in the dust, blethers on in Mass – at least
twenty years he's been with these exiled poor,
tugging their faith like a spoilt child at a dress.
He gets flustered even when he snores
in his hammock. When the children come from class
and tickle under his chin he's glad and sits
and tells of the time he saw a snake in the grass
grab a leaping frog in one gulp, like a whip
a man's arm thick – *Ah, la naturaleza*,
he beams, his eyes alight, his gaze fixed
already on a sermon about nature's beauty
and its terror. The children run away to lunch.
Later, in the evening, the tired padre
wanders house to house, at least among
his favourites, chatters with the women
who give him coffee in their unchipped mugs.
First up every morning, his duty makes him
driver of the teenagers to the local school
ten miles away along dirt tracks that wake them
soon enough with potholes large as mortars'
blasts; he laughs as they bounce and cry, *Ay, padre!*,
clucks and flaps when stuck in muddy water
after rains. At Mass he tells his parables
of Christ's love – the image of a mother
bearing home her drunken son, the terrible
look on her face, is one, he says, which stays
with him. With that, he raises arms outstretched,
pauses for effect, bends his frown and prays.

TOWN DRUNK, SAN MARCOS

He slouches, shirt-less; with slow-motion blinks
sways where he stands, holding a wooden post.
He scratches a scar, a badge inflamed on his chest,
staggers, stretches his arm like an oar, slips
backwards, flapping the air like water, sinks
on buckled legs. *Comprame una bolsa de agua,*
he shouts. I buy the water in a plastic bag
which he sups like a sleepy baby on a nipple
before it spills, dribbles down his stubble,
splashes in the dust around his bloody feet

and washes me away to infancy, to a seat
in a sunlit city park where I watch a man,
pointing the way for his drunken eyes to follow,
brush a rosehead and scatter petals in a halo
round his shoes and hold his shaking hand
to my mother, asking for a fare as if a bus
at that moment is drawing up beside us,
its tyres studded with petals from the roses it has crushed.

SIGNING

the language of touch, the speechless
vocabulary of hands.
'Request' by Norman McCaig

From your signing class you show me *giraffe* and *camel*.
You show me *I want* and *I do not want*.
I want to ask for *give* and *take*, which you know well,
your hands sweeping like swallows,
but I'm scared you'll just give me the usual two fingers,
a quick stab upwards with the 'V'
and a smirk that says everything.

My hands speak their own language,
whispering the names of unknown animals
and strange desires on the sounding board of your body.
But you correct my fingers' grammar,
making my hands clumsy as hammers
as you fall asleep to dream of words sculpted in the air
until I wake you, signing *water* on your face.

BEING GEORGE FOX

There may be two sides
                              to everything.

But I think
              I can be trusted
          to know

                                        my Rift
              from my Light.

                    *

The supermarket is full of mothers
trailing children down the aisles,
scanning red-eyed torches over frozen dinners.
Everyone avoids eye- and trolley-contact.
The announcer's mumble you haven't been listening to
cuts off with that spine-freezing white-noise
you always get in comedies when the nervous hero
takes the mike but can't begin, and suddenly
another voice is ministering over the tannoy. Mine.
It isn't coded strips the inner-laser scans!
I scream – *Ignore the cut price salvations!*
At first you expect young assistant managers
and the one bored uniform over at the booze
to come running, mad at this intrusion,
desperate to prevent this villainy continuing.
But no one's noticed... And you're worried now. You're frightened.
Abandoning your week's provisions by the cereals
you make the exit just in time to leave
madness trailing after you, frustrated yet again,
but not before you pass a 2-for-1
on Chardonnay and a woman at the end of her tether
who slaps her tiny thin-lipped child
beneath a sign that says **Cash Only**.

16

*

They told me she was staying in Lancashire.
Some clinic or other.
She hadn't eaten for twenty-two days.

When I arrived her father told me
the paparazzi were closing in
despite the staff's discretion.

I stepped into her room and was surprised
to see her sitting at the window
where the freesias' stems in a vase
looked stronger than her arms.
The petals brighter than her eyes.

She spoke of nothing but food from her past.
Sweets. The memory of lemon cake.
And strangest of all, a doctored brownie she'd smuggled
into her final Final and eaten with half an hour to go. . .

Coming down, she told me, she'd felt
like the man who flew to Moscow
undetected by the Russian radars.
Landing in Red Square in his tiny model plane
how could he not feel the wonder
and the folly of it all, she said,
as the uniforms encircled him with rifles raised?

ROAD MOVIE

We slip along the Granton shore road at sunset,
dreaming of the flight we'll take next week
to Victoria and the road trip on Vancouver Island.
We've the flat to clean and your mum and dad
to say goodbye to, the dollars to buy, the fortune
to spend in Boots on factor-15 and repellent,
the water to switch off, the video to set
for NYPD Blue, The Sopranos, Friends.

A plane heads for home as we do, its line
of billowing entrails blooming in the heavy air
reminding me of the comet's tail in the film
we saw yesterday where the earth's destroyed but isn't,
where the earth's actually America, but the President's black
so that's OK, Africa and Europe somehow
all sewn up in him and the foreign father
of the newsreader who looks like Sharon Stone.

The line burns red in the setting sun,
then cools to blue as the summer night begins.
I want a sudden jump-cut now to send us
to The Schooner in Tofino, the mist on Long Beach,
the feast and candlelight at Point No Point,
but I flashback to the car instead, the silence
now the plane has passed broken when you sigh,
"I'm glad it's Canada we're going to and not the States."

THE HOUSE SWAP

It was all done through Rotary and we were able
to swap with a family in Boston. I cut the grass
and Jane bought new cutlery and a microwave.
She wanted to give the whole house a face-lift
but I told her it'd cost more than the holiday.
I couldn't get her to relax. We slept the last night

in the spare room but she had another night-
mare so we were up early and able
to make the airport well before midday.
I was terrified that Jane would start to regress
in some way, and she could tell. "The break'll lift
my spirits - don't worry," she said - but a wave

of panic rolled through me when she waved
to two boys in the concourse and called, "Good night!"
when the parents ushered them into a lift,
the father glaring at us. We found a table
by a huge window and stared at the strips of grass
between the runways shimmering in the heat of the day.

We landed at the same time on the same day
that we'd left and I felt as if our own heat-wave
had travelled with us when I saw the same burnt grass
and floating tarmac. Jane slept that night
but I couldn't. The heat and the worry were unbearable
so I decided to explore the house, having left

a note on the pillow. Quietly I started to lift
the covers they'd draped, as if for some birthday
surprise, in the spare rooms they weren't able
to lock - but in the children's room a wave
of nausea and guilt stopped me and I sat all night
among the white shrouded shapes like gross

snowmen, melting. At daybreak I looked at the grass
and the long shadows and thought of the twins in the chair-lift
on our last holiday, the photo of us all the night
they buried me in snow, and then the day
of the accident. I wept and a cover shook in a wave
as I gripped it, but the tears were for Jane and for me. I was able

to see we'd both regressed until we were left
wavering siblings to each other like night
and day, without a home and inconsolable.

CAMPING ON THE FAULT

A rock broke free and like two stowaways
we camped there drifting northwards on Point Reyes.

One day I left you sleeping and walked through a maze
of pines where I saw a fox which turned and watched me
inching forward, its eyes never off me,
until it backed away into the shade;

which is just what I did when I found you lying on the beach
and you didn't see me and your open hands reached
not to wave or beckon me but to catch the heat.

In the dusk I stalked you all the way to the tent.

Like fires on a skyline the eyes of raccoons glinted
from the brush as my own eyes there on the severed rock
looked at you on the other side of the fault
when you eased away, staring straight ahead.

GULF WAR AT NOTRE DAME

The Golden Dome glitters on the skyline
and the exact replica of Lourdes Grotto is dotted with candles.
Young American virgins, with hairstyles
that defy gravity, are praying to God and His Mother
while the C.I.A. recruitment officer, nipping
between here and Mormon Utah, intones
Gad, Cuntry, Nohder Dayme,
knowing well that blind devotion makes
God's Own the best usurpers of democracy.

In the stadium the crowd salutes a goatee'd midget
turning somersaults beside the cheerleaders.
Everyone is blessed by The Touchdown Jesus
on the library wall. The war, too, is a football game.
Perfect passes end with snow on the screen
and a cut to the commentator, breathless.
Yellow ribbons flutter in the trees like flags
and the Scuds must be dropping on South Bend itself:
in the survival store down town

the gas–masks have all sold out.

THE SENTENCE
after Nora Mendez, El Salvador

Don't think I haven't imagined your face
escaping from my fingers, breathing secret whispers.

Don't think I haven't felt the force
of your name inside my head, demanding its space.

Don't think I can't use the defence
that everything I do for you has its own law.

Above all, when you find yourself protesting,
when a sea floods your cheeks and you can't sleep,
when you've turned my words into slogans against me,
don't think I've forgotten we're condemned to love.

IONA

Four of us crammed together on a bench after the pub,
laughing at farting cows and blaming Ewan.
We craned our necks to see the meteors fall –
I forget how many there were or what we wished for
but I remember innumerable stars that didn't move
and the whiteness laced through the constellations
which I thought was just a smudge on my glasses
until you cried out, "Look, you can see the Milky Way!"

AMÉRICA
for Rigoberta Menchú and La Comunidad Nueva Esperanza, El Salvador

All the earth is a grave and nothing escapes it;
nothing is so perfect that it does not descend to its tomb. . .
Filled are the bowels of the earth with pestilential dust
once flesh and bone, once animate bodies of men
who sat upon thrones, decided cases, presided in council,
commanded armies, conquered provinces,
possessed treasure, destroyed temples,
exalted in their pride, majesty, fortune, praise, power.
Vanished are these glories, just as the fearful smoke vanishes
that belches forth from the infernal fires of Popocatepetl.
Nothing recalls them but the written page.

Hungry-Coyote (Netzahualcoyotl)
King of Texcoco 1431-72

Return to El Mozote

Expert diggers of the dead are brushing bones,
their pit protected from the sun by canvas
stretched across a skeleton of wooden slats.
We reach a metal shape that holds a plaque
assuring us THEY DID NOT DIE; THEY ARE WITH US
AND ALL HUMANITY, a silhouette of a family,
a monument that stands beneath a cross on stones
where I think the village chapel used to be
before we burned it down and hid the dead.
Some cows chewing thistles rest in shade.

Days before we mowed them down we warned
the peasants to move. They said they hadn't helped
the guerrillas, gave us soup and a supply of corn
for the whole battalion, thought they'd not be hurt,
being Protestants, odd ones out in Morazán –
'balanced like beams across the shoulders of the war,'
the pastor told us, smiling – and so they stayed.
The jefe knew a bluff when he heard one but played

a waiting game while the neighbouring villages fled.
Then, near Christmas, we struck; and hid the dead.

The Truth Commission men walk round the grave.
I'm told to fetch the jeep; I salute and leave.
One survived who heard her children plead
but bit her tongue and hid in thorns and knew
she was the one who'd been chosen to tell the truth
which is there, unearthed, the evidence amnesties
and Peace Accords will bury. THEY DID NOT DIE;
THEY ARE WITH US – I laugh and shake the keys
and kick the crowns off thistles. The truth? It lies.
There. On the tongues of lazy cattle under trees.

*

The Book Of The People

A Spanish priest translates the Popol Vuh
and catches fever. The words mutate and snake
across the page like smoke; twenty voices
chant the secret Quauhtlemallan legends
from between the covers which have turned to bark.

*

Rigoberta's First Visit To The City

With your humble, starving father you sold willow.
You saw him bow in offices to puffed-up men
who peered from machines that trapped words on wood,
square tortillas streaked with beans of ink.

The rest of the week you trekked the unknown streets
like the time in the woods when your dog ran away, too hungry
to lead you home, and you'd nothing but twigs to chew.

Your father bought you ice he couldn't afford,
its numbness a mystery hunger couldn't ruin.
All the way home in the covered truck, penniless
and gaunt, you slept, dreaming of typewriters and snow.

*

The Wooden Men Are Banished

Before the maize-paste was human-shaped
the men of wood were kings and ruled badly.

One day, everything got its revenge.

The small animals and the large animals,
the earthen jars and griddles,
the plates and pots and grinding stones,
all rose up and spoke
and smacked the faces of the wooden men.

Treat us like this and we'll rip you to shreds,
they said as they ripped them to shreds.

The stones of the fire exclaimed,
You built us up and cooked on us!

The griddles and pots shouted,
You put us on the fire and blackened us!

The houses bellowed,
You lived in us and warmed in us!

Then all together,
And you didn't even ask our permission!

*

The Seasons

The heat beats down in both the wet and dry
on Usulutan's southern coastal plain.
Its sound is the insects' pitch, the constant cry
that buzzes in the air and raps the ear with pain.
In the drought, the dust, a packet-mix
for later rain to soup, obscures the land.
Pot-holed water traps the village trucks
like armadillos when malaria, hatched in these ponds,
arrives with the rain; green erupts from the dust
and corn pokes its fingers through the ground,
reaching up for men to snap its wrists.
At night the lightning revives the rusty land
where nature delicately holds the reasons
for suffering this weather and these seasons.

*

Easter in Momostenango

Good Friday has come and I'm in the square,
rum in my pocket, the sun in my hair.
The crowds throw candles and offer me cigars;
the church is empty and so are the bars
for everyone has come to pray for my grace,
even Mary and her Son who take second place
to me, San Simón, who leads the parade
without any fuss or a priest's masquerade.

Soon I'll be burned in someone's back-yard,
away from the church where now I'm on guard –
the Son needs his moment – but I'll rise again
and be saved for a year in the brotherhood of men
who know the work of saints is hidden from their eyes
deeper in the earth than the height of the skies.

*

Flood

When the Lempa burst we camped in the cattle-shed,
our highest point. The pigs bumped their heads
and chewed the strings on the over-loaded hammocks
where the children sat as the rising water swilled.
The rain stopped when darkness fell but we watched
our backs and slept in shifts and dreamt we drifted
to a foreign land. The morning sun lifted
nothing of the water, which clutched our thighs and pulled.

I knew the crops were lost and in the end
cholera would come, but the only time I cared
was when a tarantula thought Maria was land
and climbed her leg, and she, too tired to be scared,
calmly plucked it in the dark brown sauce
which trailed its bubbles in a perfect line of dots.

*

The Disappearing Act

The boys, disguised as conjurors, went to the court
of the arrogant lords and drew crowds with tricks.

They took a dog and hacked it to bits
and when the final limb was chopped
the dog was whole. The lords came up
and told the boys to kill a servant.

The machetes swung but the scattered limbs re-formed
and the man was alive and stronger than before.

The lords were amazed and said, *Now you!*
The boys showered themselves with blows
and drenched the grass with gore. Like a dream
they appeared as before and the grass was clean.

The arrogant lords could not resist: *Kill us*
but keep us alive! The boys did the job. And paused.

The crowd waited for the resurrected
to move but the limbs just lay and bled
and the severed heads just lay and stared
at nothing and the boys just vanished in the wind.

*

Language School Outing, Quetzaltenango

The Tutor
I love to show the gringo college kids
the graves; I always stop at the wall that divides
the marble tombs of those who bought their bliss
from the mounds where babies lie unbaptised.
I tell them about the disappeared and say
at least these dead have crosses at their heads.
I love how reactions change: tears all day,
then questions on how the formal imperative ends.

The Student
I know about these crimes, but who can I blame?
He thinks we're innocents abroad and he's got
all the answers, but would he, if he asked the same
question, point the finger to this very spot?
Who fully blames his own? We're all, at best,
tourists of the dead who have no final rest.

*

The Field Of Reeds

The hawk vomited the snake;
the snake vomited the toad;
the toad couldn't vomit
for the louse stuck in its throat.

The priest looks up from the page.
He knows he sees the future
and his eyes have the fury of a saint's.

He sees five hundred years
of a people choking those
who would swallow them up; he knows
the message of their heroes
will fly beyond the page
just as the reeds will grow
which the boys planted
in the middle of their home
saying, *Do not weep,*
mother, for here we leave
the sign of our fate.

SEPTEMBER 12TH. 2001

The cold in this flat feeds the virus
which strokes me into shivers and calm solitude,
the resignation of being sick, and alive.
My illness is watery, smells of camomile.

Drops on the window eel their way down,
then dry slowly to nothing, to stains.
Traffic hisses and growls but I'm above it all
and see only ranks of chimneys on the rooves
of Leith Walk tenements and rows of windows
giving nothing of their mysteries away.

Come home quickly, Alison. Take my fevered head
in your hands, stroke my hair with tenderness
and desire, hold my slow blind kisses
to keep my eyes and lips from drying.

FLASHING AMBER

Your five-year-old fingers clutched at dials and switches
at the fair – a pilot on a carousel, you flew
from the siren wailing behind you and fixed
a steady course for the two grown-ups waving
every time you passed; but the circle spun you
from their constant place and you had to strain to see them
or learn to face ahead, knowing you were forced
to turn your back to follow the circle home
and trust, when you came around again, those arms
would still be there, waiting to lift you free.

Now you know the illusion of permanence; parents,
precious as children, grow up and leave a presence
haunting fairgrounds, children's places, crossings
where you run when the lights are flashing amber and streets
look safer on the other side, rooms where you reach
out your arms to be lifted free but your hands
find nothing but cold walls. You feel this presence
closer every day, like hearing your name
shouted in a crowd, a voice not quite your own
calling, *You can't go on like this for ever.*

THE OSTEOPATH

I drive stiffly through the rain to Auchterarder
with you beside me reading everything you can
about the First World War. Your right hand
rests on my left thigh, dips as I change gear
or leaves a sudden coolness there
on the muscle when you turn a page.
I wince and stick my belly out in pain.

The wipers sweep and click like metronomes
until I kill the engine and leave them frozen,
two blackened skulls of herons, or bayonets
fixed parallel in the middle of the glass.
You stay there reading as the windows mist
and the drips fall in bunches from the oak
I've parked under and I limp away

into a room where a skeleton hangs by the fire.
The doctor digs his fingers in my knotted flesh.
The sound of my joints popping is like distant gunfire
or splashes tapping on a metal roof.
Later, when I slide into the seat beside you,
I feel like a stone, coaxed across a frozen loch,
that shoulders through to kiss its lonely twin.

POEM WRITTEN BEFORE KNOWING OF THE TESTING OF DEPLETED URANIUM AT DUNDRENNAN

I dipped my hand in the spray
as I sailed the channel's twists from Kippford.
Rough Isle swept by and the whole Solway

opened like a map that led to Hestan's shore.
The thrashing wind and the gulls warned me off
but I found the lighthouse. I'd wanted a tower,

a flail against the darkness on the cliff
but this automaton was the squat bud of a flower,
a closed sea-anemone no one could touch.

As I sailed for home it bloomed at my shoulder.
A tentacle of light caught the wave that clutched
the stern, my wrist, then Kippford's distant shore.

THE PROGRESS OF THE PARLIAMENT

I.
I have come late to this project,
to the loud drillings, to the sight
of dinosaur-machines which stretch
their necks down into the rubble
and bring the broken stones to light.
I have come late to the stubble-
like wires jutting through the concrete,
the layers of floors that set around
the cranes which slaver and dribble
their chains to the puddled ground.

If I have to judge the progress
of something in the middle of its life
then I am caught more in the mess
of my own perception than on the wave
of some dictated zeitgeist.
So I tell myself to be brave
and crawl along the knife-
edge of my own reserved judgement,
personify some diggers and some cranes
and come to an end without a point.

II.
Climb the steps within the steps of the new glass-fronted library,
look past yesterday's obsession with the dirty work
going on immediately below and turn instead one angle upwards
to ask yourself some searching questions.
All these glass-fronted buildings – the cafes,
The Scotsman's offices, this library – are they here
to reflect the 'new transparent politics'
or show it up for what it really is – the same old same old?
And is the albino balding porcupine of Our Dynamic Earth,
itself as stark against the Crags as a dust-mite
against a giant flake of skin, rolled up in self-protection
or sniffing out the termites in the dung-hill of the Palace?
And who are you to move so quickly from yesterday's
sitting on the fence, except the lowest of the low, a citizen?

FROM A DIARY ON PORTOBELLO BEACH

A wave begins to break ten feet away.
It spills its row of dominoes and lines them up again,
too quick to see a pattern or a shape, the effort
so effortless there must be an art hidden
and precise as when a breeze just skiffs
the water so the ripples' shadows or the shadows' ripples
sweep away like herds of buffalo across a plain.

*

The beach is back after yesterday's high tide.
It survived – but sand is piled up on the Prom
where the wind shivered it across in waves all day
while at the edge of the sea the water's waves
could hardly move. They were tired little lines flopping
like fingers drumming very slowly on a desk,
as the wind whipped them back and spray took off
like flying fish and the gulls couldn't rest
but wheeled and scrawled across the turquoise-pink of dusk.
There's a huge gang of gulls today squatting
on the splayed toes of the river.
Most of them are motionless, waiting. A few bicker,
flapping lightly, until there's a sudden panic, a shower
upwards as a dog runs through them. They ripple,
then fall still again because the wind today is elsewhere.

*

There's a long low cloud from Kirkcaldy to North Berwick.
The Firth is a crumpled sheet in front of me,
pegged down by gulls like stones, hiding the sand
where yesterday two names and a heart were scored.
The sand that held those human shapes is somewhere else now -
no tide slips onto the same beach twice
as the gulls, preparing for the rain, know well.

*

A boy skiving school kicks a broken piece of wood
along the Prom towards the King's Road car park.
With every skid across the pavement more atoms
go sailing into space or into the Tides Inn.
(I wonder if the boy would get the joke if he looked.
I wonder would I feel less dizzy if I knew the point
in asking whether I like all this or I don't?)
I close my window, shutting nothing out.
Then I look more closely, then more closely still,
and see the pane is dusted with the finest motes of sand.

THE LOCUSTS IN MY REFLECTION

We were lost in Washington that summer
when the seven-year locusts sprang the traps
on Garrison Street. Flying jack-in-the-boxes
bouncing off the screen-door, they'd search the light
where we sat, arguing as usual.

I'd watch myself in the window behind you
as one by one they'd come fleeing the darkness,
smack into my furrowed brow on the glass
and drop dead out of sight. I wouldn't flinch.

They kept punching out these holes in the night,
aiming for us, the spot-lit slapstick fools.
But by September they'd given up, like us:
when the nights grew long their corpses crunched
on the pavement like popcorn under our soles.

MARGINALIA FOR AUDEN'S *ISCHIA*

There's a room here where nuns once sat their dead
on throne-latrines to rot and drip into the bowls,
believing this posture would ease their resurrection.
Disease was rife throughout that order!
But those stone chairs survived well enough
the corpses that melted – and an earthquake or two.
In another shaded vault once-brilliant frescoes
suffer in comparison. Unprotected from the artistry
of damp air and graffitists, they flake like patches
of psoriasis – half a John the Baptist reaches
to cup a nose, some vaguely coloured plaster
and a scribble from *Marco and Vittoria, 1990*.
We leave the Castello, craving a roadside pizza
and enduring art, walking the causeway which appears
in early scenes of *The Talented Mr Ripley*.

*

What would you make of the island now? You'd love
the gay couples riding their noisy scooters
past the beach's skein of German bathers
into the heat and tack of Forio. Your old haunt,
the Internazionale, would make you smile.
But soon you'd grieve. Not for La Mortella –
Susana Walton's tourist-blighted garden's
a collaboration that's survived these years
because it's natural – but for the spluttering buses
which give the choking wail of warning, the sign
that the time of darkness and outcry has indeed returned;
for all the miserable strangers slowly burning
by the Mezzatorre's pool; for the marble milestones
which you'd see have melted in the winter rain
because they were – of course – just limestone.

THE CHAPTER HOUSE, INCHCOLM ABBEY

*Stet domus haec donec fluctus formica marinos ebibat, et totum testudo
perambulet orbem. (Let these walls stand for as long as it takes an ant to
drink the ocean, and a turtle to circle the world).*
*- According to legend, this was the inscription above the Abbey's original
doorway.*

For Alison.

I want to write our *Scotichronicon*,
the legend of you saving me from the storm,
sheltering me here and sharing your one possession,
your faith, like the hermit who shared his tiny farm
of one cow and shellfish with the shipwrecked man
who was in fact the king who gave Inchcolm
its Abbey. If that sounds too pretentious, then
I'll scrap it, change the tone and start again,

but you can't deny we knew we'd marry here
when we entered the Chapter House, its perfect octagon
an ancient ring that held us like pagan worshippers
as we kissed and gently made our faces turn
so that from above we formed an eight of hair
and cheeks that crossed at our lips. If hyperbole's forbidden
I'll be as silent now as we were then
when we stopped and laughed, two nothings in ourselves again,

too scared to speak of marriage. The number eight
will lose me in its loops as I dream alone:
of two moons colliding; the snake that ate
itself; of me, aged eight, arriving home
from school to find my mother trying to tessellate
a patchwork quilt of perfect octagons
(she said you need a square to fill the gaps);
and the world that's fallen off the turtle's back...

I take it, then, you'll allow me to exaggerate!
I hope you let the sin of repetition
be forgiven, too, since I commit it – the eight
that's in everything needs double recognition.
Draw one from Porty to Dunfermline and you'll make
an 'X' across the Forth that sets its kiss on
Inchcolm Abbey so that our homes when we met
are joined through this House now and we can never forget

that all of us live on someone else's horizon. . .
The empty cups of our separate selves have kissed
and left this final perfect eight frozen
and fallen on its side as if to make a toast
to infinity which fills us slowly and then spills over.
What we drink keeps filling up like this
and whether we're a shape or a space in the endless
tessellation, we are a piece that fits.

AN EXHORTATION TO READ MICHAEL ONDAATJE'S
IN THE SKIN OF A LION

I do not wish for plot and all its consequences
but trust me: though this will take time,
there is order here, very faint, very human...

I am in Upper America, searching for lost millionaires
and catching nuns who fall from half-built bridges,
falling myself in love with women who tell me
they will leave me, and do.
                                        I work with dynamite.
I give *fee-ee* to my *gooshter*. I let herds of bullocks
snuffle with my socks in forests.
I dig beneath Great Lakes for water systems.
I am a log exploding, on fire in a river.
I am a puppet thumping on the floor for my release.
I am blindfold. If you move my nose will bleed.
If you fall my arm will break. So hold me,
paint me blue to set me free, send me to Marmora
and whisper once again those parables
of love and death –
                                        Strangers kiss as softly as moths...
I have taught you that the sky in all its zones is mortal.

All around us we will hear your words repeated,
an alien audience echoing every syllable.

THE BELL

'Quaker women [in the 17th century] espoused a plan to melt church bells
as a wealth-creation scheme.'
*– Stevie Davis, **Unbridled Spirits**.*

For The Trident Three

We chopped it down, catching the wind
on our cheeks as it fell. The cracked stone
at the base of the tower held the buckled metal
still humming. We leant against it,
hugging it, loving the deep echoes
between our ribs until we pulled away
like bits of torn skin from a swollen thumb.

The coins we minted chink in our purses now
and Sundays are silent except for the clapper
we saved from the furnace, which we smack
between collection plates like cymbals as we march
over cobbles which will ring out long after we are gone.

HISTORY
after 'Mi Pais' by Marden de Ciazo, El Salvador

My country is a book
to be read on sleepless nights.

It is a cradle,

a bleak plateau,
its hiding places empty,

a fist sleeping
in the lazy centuries.

Be careful.

Before the mountains are born
there is nothing.

PLATO IN POTOSÍ

Banished to float through time, he lives in shadow,
in every type of cave you'd care to mention
or imagine: the empty boots of cars, the cellars
of murderers, sea-worn smugglers' nests – he knows
them all, but feels most at home right here.
This place of torture's so like his own invention
it scares him, but who wouldn't be drawn to a metaphor
made real – the strange beauty of the fires
burning in the mules' eyes, on the hair between their ears,
on the slaves' glistening backs as they mine the shadows?

*

He dreams of the two young brothers in Bermuda
who, playing on their lawn, kicked a ball
as far as the garden's end but saw it fall,
before it reached the fenced-off cliff-edge, through a
hole hidden by clumps of uncut grass.
He dreams of how they parted the grass like hair
and took turns to squeeze through the gap in the ground
to see the stalactites upside down sprouting
from the rock to the cave below where tourists flock now
to stroke the dripping spikes when the guide's not looking.

*

There are times he wants to recant everything,
plead with those he would have banished; he prays
that one will come and find this abandoned mine,
pull aside the beams and the danger sign
from the hole and fall through time with every step
until she's here and says, *Come up – it's over...*
He sits in hope, perched like an angel at the top
of a seam, at the end of a whip, on the shoulders of a slave
who serves the cruel pale strangers in this cave
who live in a world where the only sun is silver.

TIMELINE

You were a wideboy flashing a forearmful of dodgy watches up a close.
You were a fist pounding on empty mines and hulls of ships.
You were the wind whistling across the jaws of Rob Roy's caves.
You led the march to Highland Games. You sold stolen Loch Ness souvenirs
at car boot sales, and smart missiles to stupid men in double-breasted suits.
Your tartan changed daily during your identity crises.
Your drunken blood ran thick as oil when you opened your veins in the bath.
They stitched you up like a Frankenstein's monster. You went North.
You made up the myths about the ferocious whipping ferns of Treshnish
and the feral hamsters of North Berwick Law.
                                        No one made up any myths about you.
You bought a calendar and filled its boxes with dreams and exclamation marks.
You left some spaces empty and they were like the gaps in your teeth
or the missing sleepers under your endless tracks.
You travelled on, laying the line as you went, and what a paradox
it was to see your future plans become the records of your past
which must be hidden now for thirty years, or another thirty after that. At least.

GENETIC ENGINEERING

A bearded man I was told was a famous tenor
ate with us once at home when I was ten.
He gave us our own private concert
and I was amazed by the spray of his saliva
when he sang. He took a great interest
in me, too, smiling at me all through dinner.
I was polite but disconcerted
until my mother told me he'd lost
a son who would have been my age by then
if he'd been alive.

And suddenly, as I imagined I was someone else's son,
I remembered the fear I felt the time my mum
assured me, *It'll grow another one,*
the lizard's tail still twitching on my palm.

ANNIVERSARY
after Tomaz Salamun

My tears drop into the spilt milk – split! split!
How can I get used to this white madness?
It hates its own shape and takes that of the floor,
the skirting boards, the kitchen walls.
As the milky tears rise, I realise my new shoes
from Russell and Bromley, a gift from my husband,
given in guilt for all the recent hurt,
will be ruined. I curse my stupidity.

I know I could open the door to him but why
let the milk take us both? As he screams,
as he hammers at the door, and as I drown,
I imagine the stretcher-bearers' sodden footprints
through the hall and down the steps to the ambulance.
The snow you tread is always the last to melt.

FRISBEE

It's dusk beneath the castle rock,
her favourite place for this game.
The golden statue by the lawn
surveys the rhododendrons' shadows.
I'm free again from her cupboard's dust.

I can't make sense of this emotion
behind her flowing arm and snapping wrist
that makes me bruise the ball of his thumb
when he fails to catch me cleanly, or this
behind his throw that slings me
over her head.

There's more than friendship
in his wayward pass into the bushes
that sends them together to hunt me down.
And there's less than love in her pointing –
"There it's!" – just to turn her back
and step again onto the lawn.

I can't make sense of it;
but I know my essence lies in the gap,
like this, between two people.
I'm just hollow plastic
but I cut through silences.

Back in the game,
when I cross the space
between her chest
and his bruised hand,
I catch the fading light
and fly.

'I POUR WET LEAVES'

I pour wet leaves onto the fire
and thicken the smoke in the low-sun evening sky.
I think of new popes, and Luther
on the *Scala Santa*, climbing the treadmill of devotions,
praying for an ancestor to be released from Purgatory –
the story goes it was on the last stair,
after years of glowing, that the ember lit
the fire in his head, revealing Faith Alone.

I offer more leaves and my own prayer,
not for ancestors but descendants.
It is dark now. Only God can see the colour
of the smoke or know the good it will do me
and what steps I have to take to stand
on solid ground again and trust it.

POTENTIAL

You remember how you loved those lessons in Physics
about energy and acceleration – men like sticks
standing at the tops of cliffs or stairs, the stunted
awkward trolleys that collided, or shunted
sadly down a ramp after 'an explosion',
the strips of ticker-tape that flowed on
and on like threads unravelling. . . Everything
was movement, heat, or hidden force that hung

suspended just by standing still.
So now it's strange that you forget the hill
you struggle up has heat inside it that's lost
to you forever, and climbing's not
a movement forward, but just a way to stall
the inevitable, endless, capacity to fall.

'I FOUND SOMETHING'

I found something I couldn't name.
It was a tree, certainly. It had branches and bark
but the patterns on the leaves were like veins gone berserk
and it was strange how I felt the same
wrenching emptiness inside me every time
I left it. At first I didn't have the heart
to tell the little man my secret, and there's a part
of me that would have liked to keep him in his dream
because we're different now.
The twig without its fruit is like a scar
and I feel like an actor writing the scene
as I play it. I draw my finger along the furrow
on his brow as he tries to understand what I mean
when I say that we're at war.

THE BLACK BOX

The plane is delayed on its journey home –
the minutes are caught in a tight black box.
From the air the village is an orange comb,
the winking lights like tiny static shocks.
The pilot reports the weather as the engines hum –
the box digests every word he speaks.
Beyond the lights the ocean's darkness looms
like a black hole. The waves draw and flex
but in the sky everything is calm –
the radio whispers and the tail-light blinks.
When the lights go out and the radio falls dumb
the static and the voice will be forever in the box,
but for now the plane is delayed on its journey home
while deep in the belly sleeps the bomb.

THE WAR ON *TERROR*

"This must be a war on terror, as an abstract noun and as a universal policy." (Michael Gove, The Times, 16.10.01)

The first bombardment missed completely
and the uniformed spinners were forced to 'express regret'
for the loss of *pleasure* and *enthusiasm*.
Faith, *Hope* and *Love* were quickly whisked
away to an underground bunker on St Kilda
while *vengeance*, *fury* and *diplomacy*
were issued with radiation suits and gas-masks.
The bombing continued, always at night
when *deceit* and *cowardice* work best.
The targeting slowly improved.
Soon that first 't' was toppled and the broadsheets
enjoyed playing with the word *error* that remained
(more shaken than usual it has to be said).
"Progress is being made," the talking heads
assured us when the final 'r' was reduced to rubble,
but the double that remained, pouched so securely
between those vowels, weren't much fun to play with
and even the tabloids began to express concern
over the length of the campaign... The war continued
but news became less frequent, somehow less focused.
We started to forget what *terror* had actually meant
and went on with daily life with meagre *fear*
and *panic* in our midst. It was only much later
we were told how nouns could change their shape
after such an assault, could drop a consonant
or morph a vowel, add a suffix or superlative
or even clone themselves in foreign languages.
They didn't tell us all the forms *terror* had taken,
but someone leaked the final transformations
and we saw *sorrow* weeping in the dust
and *zero* naked as an orphan and finally
Terra Firma, *La Tierra*, the *Earth* itself
standing shoulder to shoulder in the smoking rubble.

MANIFESTO

Our patience will not yield, our resolve will not break.
We will liberate our children's minds.
We will protect their innocent hearts.
Our strong actions will follow our strong words.
The thirsty will drink, the hungry will eat.
We will teach you to believe what you read.

We will teach you to believe what you read.
Our patience will not yield, our resolve will not break.
The thirsty will drink, the hungry will eat.
We will liberate our children's minds.
Our strong actions will follow our strong words.
We will protect their innocent hearts.

We will protect your innocent hearts.
You will learn to believe what you read.
Strong actions will follow these strong words.
Our patience will not yield, our resolve will not break.
We will liberate our children's minds.
The thirsty will drink, the hungry will eat.

The hungry are drunk, the thirsty may eat.
We will not betray their innocent hearts.
We will not enslave our children's minds.
They will never disbelieve what they read.
Our patience will not yield, our resolve will not break.
Strong actions first demand strong words.

Strong actions first demand strong words
like, *If the thirsty drink and the hungry eat*
our patience will not yield, our resolve will not break.
We will not betray the innocent heart
of this manifesto – believe what you read.
Read my lips: we will enslave your children's minds.

To free them, we must enslave your children's minds.
The actions of the strong speak louder than their words –
if you refuse to believe what you read,
the thirsty won't drink, the hungry won't eat.
We will protect our innocent hearts.
We have patience. You will suffer, yield, break.

We will read your hungry minds.
We will break your strong, strong hearts.
You will eat our innocent words.

THE CROWD

Beside the museums and the ice cream stalls,
beside the vendors with their painted silk,
their wooden carvings, their mirrors framed
by silver fish, three performers stand
in the centres of three circles. At the edges
of these spaces the crowd lingers.
Behind the lingering crowd is the crowd that moves ceaselessly,
sliding past itself, slowing the circles like damaged cogs.
An act picks up momentum – fire–breathing
on a unicycle, juggling blades blindfold –
and the movement turns to a trickle.
An act ends, a new performer takes the patch
in some unspoken, unseen queue,
and the cogs whirl into overdrive, oiled suddenly.
And so it goes... Until the fight begins, late in the hot afternoon.
In a yawning circle left unguarded as accomplices
are pulled, unwilling, to a show, a couple appear,
blind to the line they've crossed. Before they can be joked away,
the man begins to shout, there in the centre of the O.
You useless fuckin cunt. Ah telt ye, Ah telt ye,
and still ye couldnae fuckin dae it, could ye?
Fuckin hoor – dinnae look at me lik that, ye cunt.
The performer does her best to cope, walking round them
in mock confusion and disgust, but they're oblivious,
and now she's lost the crowd which shifts and murmurs
at the growing anger and abuse. The woman stares
at a point above the heads that watch her.
The pale skin of her face is taut, her lips are thin and quivering.
She says nothing which makes the man more furious
so he jerks and swings her like a soldier's dummy,
until, of course, he hits her with an open–handed slap
that sends her to the ground where she sobs and holds her face.
The crowd is triggered, moves between the woman's
body and the man, who has begun to step, crouched
and spitting through his shouts, towards her.

He screams over these bodies, through them,
ignoring them as if they're a fence he can't be bothered
to climb. *You fuckin cunt!* he shouts. *Ah'm gonnae fuckin kill ye.*
D'ye hear me? D'ye hear me, cunt?
The crowd has picked the woman up, helps her as she turns
from the growing wall that blocks him.
He stares at her back until she disappears
and his voice drops slowly till he's whispering,
D'ye hear me? D'ye hear me? to the distance, to himself,
to the line of blank and silent faces that encircle him.

SILK FLOWERS

The back of the fridge, still hidden by your flowers,
hums a broken tune to the shelf where pictures,
cups and pots sit back to back like drinkers
in a crowded bar. The clock ticks in the kitchen

and gathers dust which holds your skin
mingled with my own, the only remnant of us
now the last photos are binned. The word *conversion*
echoes in my head, and I hear *...version, ...version*

and me chopping onions as fast as I can
before the tears come, showering affection
on you as useless as rain on silk flowers,
needing the grace of a God who isn't jealous.

Now I want flowers that die within a week,
given by a sinful lover who knows they deserve
light and who keeps our hearts' dirty machinery
open, knowing we can mend it only if we look.

THE NET

The Beer Expert on *I Love 1995*
is talking about alcopops. Names like *Hooch*
and *Two Dogs, Purple Turtle, Sick-in-a-Minute*
trip from his lips in a litany of post-ironic
retro-kitsch. His grin before they cut him off
belongs in *The Ship and Whale* after work
(or *The Three Compasses, The Cock and Monkey,
The Nobody's Inn*) at the moment his wife walks in
to show him her latest black-and-whites – cobbles
in close-up in an alley in Paris, the grill
on a vent, frost on a cobweb in Windermere.

Leaving the studio he daydreams, pictures
the pub they'll open in later life on a river
somewhere in England. They'll specialise
in Trappist brews from Belgium and CAMRA-endorsed
ales called *Shepherd's Crotch* and *Weirdy-Beard's.*
They'll christen it *The Net* after her finest piece
which'll hang on the longest wall, a blown-up shot
in sepia of a net on a pier just after dawn,
a giant empty board for the game of *Go*
before the counters hook, like water-drops,
on linking corners, before the strategies begin.

He walks through London in this dream-time,
these moments when the real thinking gets done,
when the future's clear as her photographs and lives
in the gaps of zebra-crossings, the flight of stones
skimmed across the Serpentine, the rhythmic
flick of the pub-door after lunch, when the present's
peopled by cameos – the sudden tug of a traveller
garrotting his rucksack, the shock of a shopkeeper
dressing a dummy – and when the past is a dark-room
empty of her negatives, where he can't tell the difference
between what's caught and what keeps falling through.

PEACE HOUSE, BY DUNBLANE

I.
This is a den where protesting angels
sip non-violence like Gaelic coffee.
The sea-salts of Faslane and Iona fleck the carpet.
There in the corner sit the guilty boots, earning a breather.
The smell of tea and pine and books drifts in the air
while plots are hatched, free-range.
They strut out of the house straight onto the road.

II.
The town is pinned to the map now
like a butterfly to paper beside a Latin name.
There are other creatures hidden somewhere,
weaving a chrysalis from the broken web between us,
hanging on the underside of our dreams.

When we least expect them
butterflies will emerge, so many butterflies
colour itself will brush our faces, sweeping fine dust
like make-up on our cheeks we'll never wipe away.
And we'll let them fly. We'll let them.

WINTER'S LAST WORD

My brother had a pen which wrote strange stories.
It wrote sonnets to his lover and lay beside the bed
when they slept entangled, head to head.

One night it wrote a riddle on the freshest page:

As I lay my dying body down
on the thawing ground I see the flowers bloom
which will wither on my breath
when I've risen, bringing another death.

We drank ourselves stupid by the fire, working it out.
I asked my brother to lend me his enchanted pen
and wrote our answer down, but out in the cold
it was already written in the fallen snow.

THE STONE

Locked across the hole,
I sat and dreamt of movement,
remembered Sisyphus. I wanted to roll
forever up and down an endless hill like that.

In my wet creases the first spores of moss
gathered – it was warm at my back
as if the deep earth breathed.
The garden watched me.

When they came it took three of them
to shift me. The cave sighed over my shoulder
and they were all sick at my foot.

They dragged the remains past me but returned
to place these bloodied hand-prints on my side,
patting me gently as if I'd done the right thing.

JOINT

His head sinks further into the cushion
as he smokes, focusing on nothing
but the cone of light that's left
after the gentle brush of ash
against the saucer on his belly.

When she's home from work exhausted
or tearful or high on a success
he's there behind her for her coat,
fleecing it for the purse
as he leads her to the couch.

Her head fills the cup his own head
has hollowed in the cushion
and she sighs as he rolls another joint.
Don't be angry, baby, he says.
Here. Toke on this. Chill out.

She gazes at him as if he's from
another world. Clear as water
her eyes watch him, watch him for so long
he sinks into them, a gentle, drifting
mote that can't be followed.

EASTER

Across the stale mysterious season
the year crawls to its death. Resurrection
will be an adder-skin by a fence,
a pouch of snow discovered
in the folds and seams of these hills.

ROCKCLIFF

This crimson sea-anemone was all mouth.
Broken tendrils on the pool's floor
are spat-out useless gums,
cushions of blood. Crab-litter.
This skeleton caught
in the long grass was a meal.
The wave that broke just now
was a curled lip without a tongue.
The beach is a huge yawn
after a feast.

ISLANDS

The older I become the more
I am aware of exile. (Ron Butlin, 'Claiming My Inheritance')

Iona

The summer sand has a tourist brochure's gloss.
I leaf its sticky pages through my fingers.

Running my hands over the world like this
leaves an imprint. It marks me too,
gluing its microbes on my fingers like news-print
or pollen on the dipping head of a humming-bird
that cannot help tasting the flowers, moving
among them for what it thinks are its own ends.
Trying to read it all too closely distracts
from the simple skill of skimming – word
to word, flower to flower, longing to longing.

Sometimes I open my hand and where I thought there was nothing
atoms of everything weigh like eggs, unbroken.

Leaving Coll

Hamish, think of those seals we watched from the rocks,
their bobbing heads like dark whiskered buoys,
or the others at Feall that rocked themselves away
when we approached because we were two.
Do you think they've ever said, in seal-barks,
Think of the men we watched who came too near;
do you think when they left one of them said,
Now that we're leaving I feel a pain, like the sting
of salt-water on sun-burned skin –
I doubt it, eh? I doubt it, eh, do you?

At John Smith's Grave

An honest man's the noblest work of God

I have walked from the Abbey, through the tourist chatter,
across the cobbles on The Street of The Dead,
on a gravel path around a new wall
built only to protect the ground where you lie,
to face Fionnphort across the pure quiet water.
From here I can read the plain words on your headstone
because they've turned it the wrong way round,
upside down, like this country when you left it.

Fingal's Cave

The sea in its pool, lunging at the rock,
is the holy water in this cathedral.

I sit on an organ-pipe of stone
amidst the candle-flickers of cameras.

The air sighs through the cave
as if a door has thudded shut or blown wide open.

I look out at the bright swell
and see a collection-bowl of seaweed in the foam.

But when I feel the sudden need to pray
it's not because this place has left me small
but because I know too well the space I fill,
just how deep my footsteps cut,
and all the pain I've ever caused.

HANGING

A flag hung at half-mast.
Who had died?
"Who's died?" I asked.
You carried on
reading the paper.

A church bell rang
over the rooftops.
Who was getting married?
"Who's getting married?" I asked.
You turned the radio up.

A fire-engine whined
across the fields.
What was burning?
"What's burning?" I asked.
You turned the cooker down.

"Look, this is ridiculous," I said.
I was mad.
"Do you love me or what?"
"Wait, let me think a minute,"
you said.

FROM MARTHA SIMMONDS' JOURNAL

The worshippers huddle as if around a fire.
Someone wets them with his words and faces open
to that rain or remain shut tightly but listening
until the silence nestles down again,
like a dog dreaming of water, into their laps.

The practised listeners are still; they welcome the warmth
of hearing nothing and smile. I push at it,
stand to let it fall, restless for sound,
eager to escape the white-noise in my head,
the bright distraction of the world after rain.

*

After white water, the river's deep slow currents
drift under vacant skies to a branch around an island
where a trunk has fallen to the nearest bank.
I cross it now before the floods sweep this bridge away
to violent falls and then vast hazes of a ghostly sea. . .

*

My words are ghosts that whisper like a drizzle.
But each thump of my pulse is a wave breaking through me –
I have been swept to a shore I thought
could not be reached. Only my dreams can drown me.

*

This was my dream. . . As darkness fell I saw a hawk hanging
on the thread of the wind. One of the lambs cried out.
At dawn the storm ceased without warning,
the sun lighting the clouds like glowing coals.
I found the lambs alive. Beside them
the hawk's twisted carcass like a burst pillow.

*

Each fevered breath I take from the world's thin crown
is just another blow on loaded dice.
My heart is slow and my eyes are closed
to the Light Within that I will never own.

Your laugh cracks in the air between us.
Your eyes' crystals glisten like drops of dew
in the morning of your face. I bend close,
breathe in your ear, *You are my God.*

I have yet to discover
the place where one thing ends
and another begins does not exist –
ministry and prayer, acting Jesus
and claiming you're the Christ,
words and the lips that shape them,
those lips and those they kiss
and those they'll never kiss again.

In the distance today I mistook a bird
for a seal's head on the sea's thin glass.
The windless day rubbed the skyline out
and made me a foolish watcher from the window.

You could say I mistook you for water
in the dusty air of my love for you –
you drained away when I moved too close.
I should have stayed still, thirsting.
You would have vanished when the light changed

but for a moment, to a distant watcher,
I could have been an imagined creature
breaking the tension on your surface
before I sank or flew away.

The world is a mirror.
No – the world is a prism
refracting and reflecting heaven
to my eyes that only see in colour.
I look at, say, the sea, at any hour –
the world is indifferent –
and what I see is just a fragment
of the dimmest star.

But when I know my portion
of the world, or find that bit of broken light
in me, I'll be drops of water, then the rainbow
passing through,
dreaming its return
to white.

NOTES

In October 1656, James Nayler, a prominent Quaker leader – second only to
George Fox – rode into Bristol surrounded by followers singing hosannahs in
deliberate imitation of Jesus' entry into Jerusalem. One of these followers
was Martha Simmonds. Nayler was later tried by Parliament for blasphemy
and, narrowly avoiding the death penalty, punished by having his tongue
bored with a hot iron, being branded with a 'B' on the forehead, and being
whipped hundreds of times on the back.

*Nayler's strange performance was something the Quaker movement definitely did
not need. It came at a particularly inopportune moment in their struggle to win
greater toleration [. . .] Fox saw from the beginning that he had to repudiate
Nayler unequivocally, as indeed he had already done before Nayler ever got to
Bristol. As he complained in a letter he sent to Nayler in Exeter jail: "Martha
Simmonds [. . .] bade me bow down, and said [. . .] my heart was rotten [. . .]
and she came singing in my face, inventing words. [. . .]"*
– Leo Damrosch, The Sorrows of the Quaker Jesus

Allan Crosbie was born in Bermuda, but grew up in Scotland. After graduating from St Andrew's University, he completed a Masters in Peace Studies at Notre Dame University in the United States during the first Gulf War. To recover from the irony, he travelled throughout Central America, including a year working with a community of repatriated refugees in El Salvador and a short spell for the UN Truth Commission in that country. He now teaches English in Edinburgh and lives with his wife Alison in Portobello.

Also by Allan Crosbie (as editor) – *Such Strange Joy: ten years of Shore Poets* (iynx publishing)